BARNS

BARNS

BARRON'S

Introduction

"Nobody knows what to make of barns…" opens Peter Davison's poem "Barn Fever," and he's quite right. Barns have the distinction of being mostly free of the architect's designing mind, and yet they fill a place in the rural landscape even larger than churches. Across the United States, barns can be seen floating on the horizon like great ships on the sea. They are utterly practical constructions, and yet there is something undeniably romantic about them. Living barns are maternal—always working, storing, or sheltering—and the cultivation of the land surrounding them is entirely dependent on their presence and efficiency. Barns can evoke childhood imagination, adolescent romance, or the regular aisles, pens, and stalls of the mature mind. But the barn has grander power, too. It represents the Jeffersonian ideal of a rural people's state, a Protestant wholesomeness, and the belief that hard work will be rewarded.

Davison's poem continues to question the value we should give these structures once they no longer "shelter anything we value." The indirect answer follows—"Without the barn there

would be little cause / to call this piece of land more than a piece / of land." In other words, the barn gives the land a *history* and an *identity*. It has a function beyond the functional. In a country that has seen so much change in a relatively short history, the American barn is iconic.

However, to call a barn "American" is to simply limit it to geographical and cultural terms. Barns come in all shapes and sizes, not to mention ethnicities—there are English barns, Dutch (or German) barns, Swedish barns, Finnish barns, Italian barns, Ukrainian barns…the list goes on. There are round barns, multifaceted barns, and barn-shaped barns. When you think about it, the American barn is no different from the American him- or herself, and no more easily described.

The first American barns were either English, Dutch, or Swiss by design. But different environmental conditions in this country required changes in the approach to building them. For example, early settlers found that the raw materials available to them were superior to those found in the Old World—for example, virgin forests yielded long, straight beams that allowed for larger barns of simpler design. Also, weather conditions generally prohibited the use of thatch, so roofs and walls were sheathed in shingles.

One other aspect was different, too. In Europe, barns had been erected by those asked to do so. In America, barns tended to be raised by communities themselves. There was no feudal lord of the manor or gentleman farmer—here, communities had to rely on neighborly cooperation and voluntary service. In stylistic terms, this provided a kind of cross-pollination, producing hybrid structures unimaginable anywhere else. More importantly, it gave rise to the powerful idea of "barn-raising," a notion that has taken on metaphorical power as a way of describing any intense communal activity.

In the months following the events of September 11, 2001, there was a lot of talk of "barn-raising" as Americans worked together to overcome the devastating events of that day. Perhaps it is appropriate, then, to reflect on the images and passages that follow and realize that the image of the barn represents American strength, hope, and humanity.

A proud silhouette looming on the landscape, solitary or surrounded by ells, lean-tos, silos, or sheds, the barn commands attention, respect, even reverence. Drawn closer, the viewer's eye lingers on the rugged texture of weathered sheathing, the tilt of a weathercock pockmarked with birdshot, the repose of a listing silo, the forgotten portent of a faded hex sign.

The barn's shadows, drawn diagonally from the varied massing of volumes, beckon the curious observer around each corner. Confronted with colossal doors, he or she is forced to find a gap for a stolen peek, then to slide aside a great door for a wider look and slip inside for a survey of the cavernous interior. Only then, after the viewer's eyes adjust to the darkness, does the structure come into clear view.

Elric Endersby
Barn: The Art of a Working Building

8

The first thing you notice is the tremendous amount of space. A barn feels a lot like a church inside. Even a small one seems big because when you stand between the haylofts and look up, your view of the roof is unobstructed, save for the massive timbers that support it.

The next thing you notice is the smell—hay and manure, for sure, and perhaps, depending on the time of year, a whiff of apples or freshly split cordwood.

Something happens to the quality of light in a barn. Remember? It becomes softer, richer; it takes on the warmth of the beams.

If there are horses or cattle in the building, you can hear them moving around and sense their alert presence.

On a clear winter night, with moonlight flooding in through the open doors, you may also sense the presence of others who have been in the barn before you, the generations of families who worked in it and cherished it, the neighbors and craftsman who helped raise it a century or more ago.

Jim Doherty
"A Barn is More Than a Building. It is a Shrine to Our Agrarian Past,"
Smithsonian Magazine, August 1989

T he sun one hour from setting
    distinguishes the landscape,
so red the barn,
so white the house,
each weathered board
so cleanly defined
on the slatted grainbin,
And the hay, each mound,
and the cattle, each calf
beside each cow so singular
against a slope of golden stubble,
and the stubble, each stalk,
and along the roadside the blue-
stem, each stem, and the fenceline,
each barb, and later the moon
through the window
washing our bodies, each
member, and your hair,
under my wildest touch each
indivisible strand.

William Kloefkorn
"Nebraska, Early March"

The barn was very large. It was very old. It smelled of hay and it smelled of manure. It smelled of the perspiration of tired horses and the wonderful sweet breath of patient cows. It often had a sort of peaceful smell—as though nothing bad could happen ever again in the world. It smelled of grain and of harness dressing and of axle grease and of rubber boots and of new rope. And whenever the cat was given a fish-head to eat, the barn would smell of fish. But mostly it smelled of hay, for there was always hay in the great loft up overhead. And there was always hay being pitched down to the cows and the horses and the sheep.

E. B. White
Charlotte's Web

"There's the gate on which I used to swing,
  Brook, and bridge, and barn, and old red stable:
But, alas! the morn shall no more bring
    That dear group around my father's table;
      Taken wing!
There's the gate on which I used to swing!"

"I am fleeing!—all I loved are fled;
    Yon green meadow was our place for playing;
That old tree can tell of sweet things said,
    When around it Jane and I were straying;
      She is dead!
I am fleeing!—all I loved are fled!"

Ralph Hoyt
From "Old"

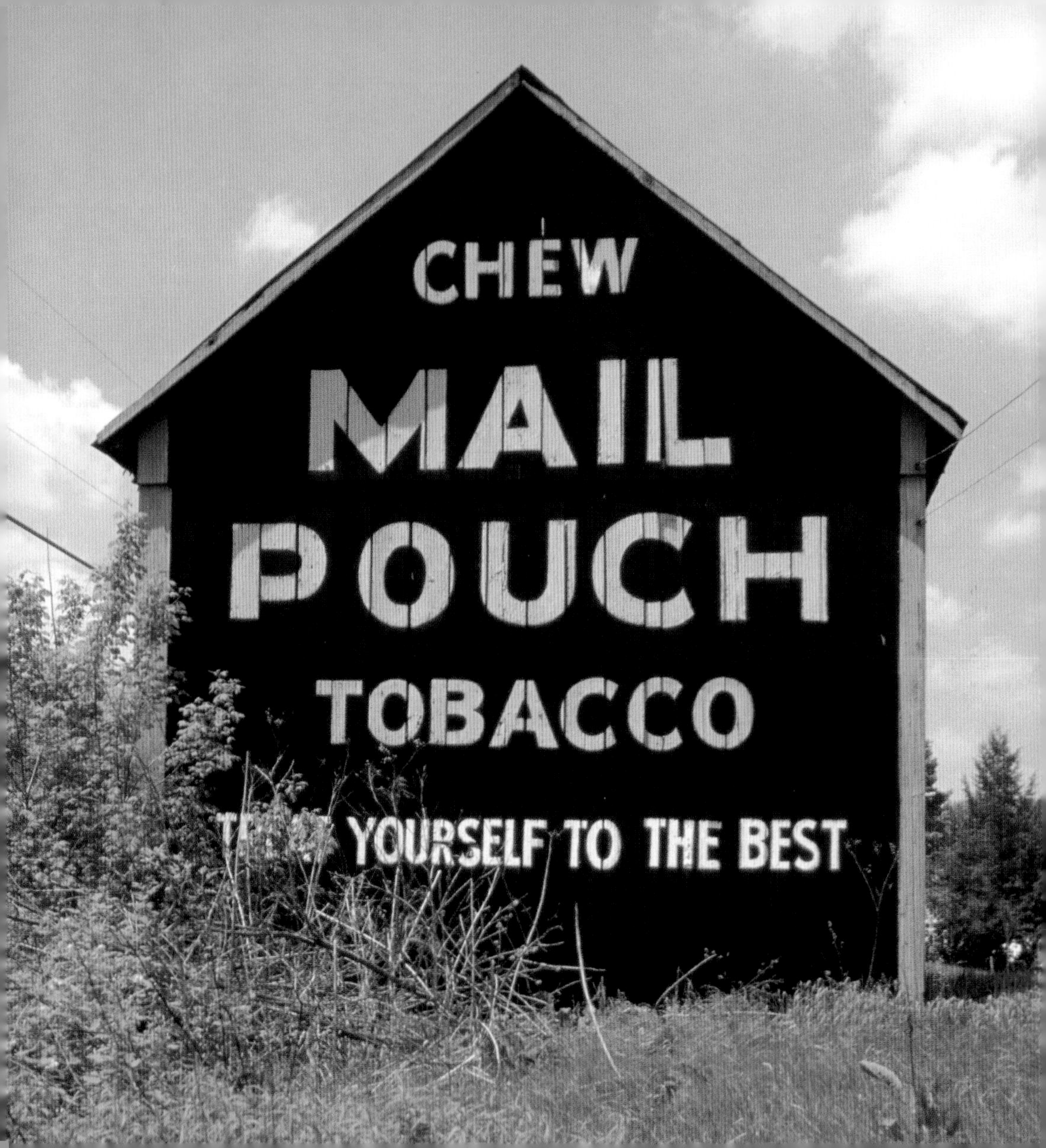
CHEW
MAIL
POUCH
TOBACCO
YOURSELF TO THE BEST

"I used to get challenged all the time. The last few years I'd show up by myself and the farmer'd come out and say to me, 'You alone? How you gonna do this without help? This one's gonna take you two days, isn't it?'"

By that time, Harley E. Warrick had painted more than 15,000 barns for Mail Pouch Tobacco and he'd yet to see one that took him two days.

"So, as I was unloading my ladder and stage, I'd ask the farmer if he had a T-bone steak he could throw on the barbeque for dinner that night." Warrick's blue eyes shown brightly under his cap. "He'd mutter something about how I'd never be finished to eat it and he couldn't see wasting good meat. By now, I'd be pulling out my ropes and pots and mops and cutters, and I'd look at the man and say, 'You just start that barbeque at 5:30. I'll be ready to eat at 6:00.' He'd walk away saying I'd never be done. And I'd just get to work."

Randy Leffingwell
"Mail Pouch Tobacco and Harley Warrick"
The American Barn

Tom asked: "Where is Grampa? I ain't seen the ol' devil."

Ma stacked the plates on the kitchen table and piled cups beside them. She said confidentially: "Oh, him an' Granma sleeps in the barn. They got to get up so much in the night. They was stumblin' over the little fellas."

Pa broke in: "Yeah, ever' night Grampa'd get mad. Tumble over Winfield, an' Winfield'd yell, an' Grampa'd get mad an' wet his drawers, an' that'd make him madder, an' purty soon ever'body in the house'd be yellin' their head off." His words tumbled out between chuckles. "Oh, we had lively times. One night when ever'body was yellin' an' a-cussin', your brother Al, he's a smart aleck now, he says: 'Goddamn it, Grampa, why don't you run off an' be a pirate?' Well, that made Grampa so goddamn mad he went for his gun. Al had ta sleep out in the fiel' that night. But now Granma an' Grampa both sleeps in the barn."

John Steinbeck
The Grapes of Wrath

Of all bird-voices, none are more sweet and cheerful to my ear than those of swallows in the dim, sun-streaked interior of a lofty barn: they address the heart with even a closer sympathy than Robin Redbreast. But, indeed, all these winged people that dwell in the vicinity of homesteads seem to partake of human nature and possess the germ, if not the development, of immortal souls. We hear them saying their melodious prayers at morning's blush and eventide.

Nathaniel Hawthorne
Buds and Bird-Voices

Per Hansa had put a great deal of thought into this matter of building a house; ever since he had first seen a sod hut he had pondered the problem. On the day that he was coming home from Sioux Falls a brilliant idea had struck him—an idea which had seemed perhaps a little queer, but which had grown more attractive the longer he turned it over in his mind. How would it do to build house and barn under one roof? It was to be only a temporary shelter, anyway—just a sort of makeshift, until he could begin on his real mansion. This plan would save time and labor, and both the house and the barn would be warmer for being together....He had a vague recollection of having heard how people in the olden days used to build their houses in this way—rich people, even! It might not be fashionable any longer; but it was far from foolish, just the same.

It will go hard with Beret, he thought; she won't like it. But after a while he picked up courage to mention his plan to her....

...House and barn under the same roof?...She said no more, but fell into deep and troubled thought....Man and beast in one building? How could one live that way?...At first it seemed utterly impossible to her; but then she thought of how desolate and lonesome everything was here and of what a comfortable companion Rosie might be on dark evenings and during the longer winter nights. She shuddered, and answered her husband that it made no difference to her whichever way he built, so long as it was snug and warm; but she said nothing about the real reason that had changed her mind.

This answer made Per Hansa very happy.

O. E. Rolvaag
Giants in the Earth: A Saga of the Prairie

Pasture-life, foddering, milking, herding,
and all the personnel and usages,
The plum-orchard, apple-orchard,
gardening, seedlings, cuttings, flowers, vines,
Grains, manures, marl, clay, loam, the
subsoil plough, the shovel, pick, rake, hoe,
irrigation, draining,
The curry-comb, the horse-cloth, the halter,
bridle, bits, the very wisps of straw,
The barn and barn-yard, the bins, mangers,
mows, racks...

Walt Whitman
From "A Song for Occupations"

When far away o'er grassy flats.
    Where the thick wood commences.
The white-sleeved mowers look like specks
    Beyond the zigzag fences.

And noon is hot, and barn-roofs gleam
    White in the pale blue distance.
I hear the saucy minstrels still
    In chattering persistence.

Christopher Pearse Cranch
From "The Bobolinks"

Farmers protected their weatherboards with what lay to hand: a mixture of red oxides from their soil, linseed oil from their flax crop, and casein from the milk of their cows. This "homegrown" paint ranged in color from bright red to purplish brown, depending on the level of iron oxide present in the local clay. All these shades of red and brown are now known generically as "barn red."...It is not possible, from a colorist's point of view, to pinpoint an actual barn red shade, but this is ultimately not important. Local variations only add to our romantic fascination with barns. One thing is certain, however: no matter how imprecise the term may be, barn red has firmly entrenched itself as the most distinctive color of the American countryside. Set against the verdant green of an American summer or the pristine white of a snowbound American winter, barn red is an enduring visual icon of rural America.

Herbert Ypma
American Country

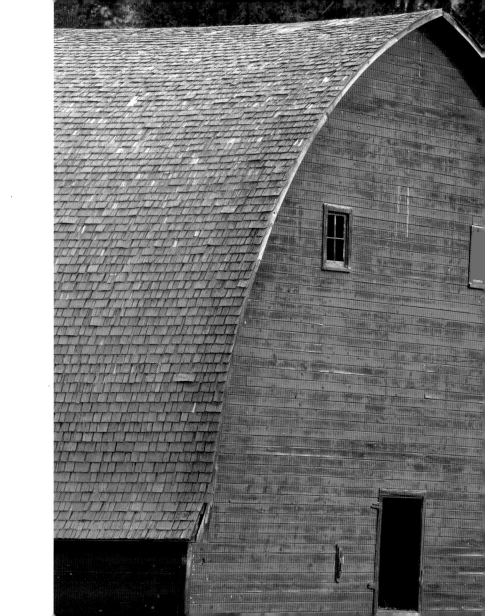

Rebuked, she turned and ran
uphill to the barn. Anger, the inner
arsonist, held a match to her brain.
She observed her life: against her will
it survived the unwavering flame.

The barn was empty of animals.
Only a swallow tilted
near the beams, and bats
hung from the rafters
the roof sagged between.

Her breath became steady
where, years past, the farmer cooled
the big tin amphorae of milk.
The stone trough was still
filled with water: she watched it
and received its calm.

So it is when we retreat in anger;
we think we burn alone
and there is no balm.
Then water enters, though it makes
no sound.

Jane Kenyon
"Portrait of a Figure Near Water"

Do not let a flattering woman coax and wheedle you and deceive you; she is after your barn.

Hesiod
Works and Days, 373

T here were some pieces of rusted tin lying out across the short pasture grass in front, remnants of the tornado of '84 that sucked the two-story barn up howling and spewed it back into thousands of pieces, and it was still lying here and there. Once in a while you'd run over a piece of it....

In winter the cattle are warm and happy in a well-lighted barn, a vast cathedral of timbers and stalls, racked hay, a tack room, a vaccination pen, a calving pen, a dehorning pen, a catch pen built of heavy pipe.

There is a cat—several cats—to keep the barn free of rodents and a few wandering chickens to pick up the ticks and fleas. The great center hall of the barn is loud late at night with the sound of Billy Ray's boots on the concrete, for there will be no slipping and sliding here in mud while trying to deliver a calf. Electric lights will furnish the brilliance required to work on mothers in trouble.

Larry Brown
Billy Ray's Farm

We put it off, not having to prove
we were Hercules, but the day came
(as it always does with work not done)
when we took our forks, spit on our hands,
hung our coats on a nail and started.
All winter the calves tramped straw bedding
to hard packed manure with a yellow smell,
tied in with straw and two feet thick,
every forkful strained our shoulders,
with every forkful we grew thick grass
on meadows where we spread this waste
from the farm's gut, remains of corn and hay
back to the fields again. It was a place
of odors, incense to bless the land,
we tugged, pulled, swore, joked,
stained with sweat and our slippery loads,
dregs of harvest for another harvest.
A spring day on the wheel of seasons.
When the pen was clean we smelled to high heaven,
lame in our muscles, weary beyond rest,
we picked up our coats, banged the forks
into their racks, made our bed on a
bale of hay, heard for applause
a banging barn door.

James Hearst
"Cleaning the Barn"

Really the children do have an ideal time out here, and it is an ideal place for them. The three sets of cousins are always together. I am rather disconcerted by the fact that they persist in regarding me as a playmate. This afternoon, for instance, was rainy, and all of them from George, Ted, Lorraine and Ethel down to Archibald, Nicholas and Quentin, with the addition of Aleck Russell and Ensign Hamner, came to get me to play with them in the old barn. They plead so hard that I finally gave in, but upon my word, I hardly knew whether it was quite right for the President to be engaged in such wild romping as the next two hours saw. The barn is filled with hay, and of course meets every requirement for the most active species of hide-and-seek and the like. Quentin enjoyed the game as much as any one, and would jump down from one hay level to another fifteen feet below with complete abandon.

Theodore Roosevelt
"Loves and Sports of the Children; Letter to Miss Emily T. Carow, Oyster Bay, August 6, 1903."
Theodore Roosevelt's Letters to His Children

The Sky is low—the Clouds are mean.
A Traveling flake of Snow
Across a Barn or through a Rut
Debates if it will go—

A Narrow Wind complains all Day
How some one treated him
Nature, like Us is sometimes caught
Without her Diadem.

Emily Dickinson
"The Sky is low—the Clouds are mean"

Just before we left Bethlehem, eleven farmers, who had been driven from their plantations by the Indians, came to me requesting a supply of firearms, that they might go back and fetch off their cattle. I gave them each a gun with suitable ammunition. We had not march'd many miles before it began to rain, and it continued raining all day; there were no habitations on the road to shelter us, till we arriv'd near night at the house of a German, where, and in his barn, we were all huddled together, as wet as water could make us. It was well we were not attack'd in our march, for our arms were of the most ordinary sort, and our men could not keep their gun locks dry. The Indians are dextrous in contrivances for that purpose, which we had not. They met that day the eleven poor farmers above mentioned, and killed ten of them. The one who escap'd inform'd that his and his companions' guns would not go off, the priming being wet with the rain.

Benjamin Franklin
The Autobiography of Benjamin Franklin

The house had gone to bring again
To the midnight sky a sunset glow.
Now the chimney was all of the house that stood,
Like a pistil after the petals go.

The barn opposed across the way,
That would have joined the house in flame
Had it been the will of the wind, was left
To bear forsaken the place's name.

No more it opened with all one end
For teams that came by the stony road
To drum on the floor with scurrying hoofs
And brush the mow with the summer load.

The birds that came to it through the air
At broken windows flew out and in,
Their murmur more like the sigh we sigh
From too much dwelling on what has been.

Yet for them the lilac renewed its leaf,
And the aged elm, though touched with fire;
And the dry pump flung up an awkward arm;
And the fence post carried a strand of wire.

For them there was really nothing sad.
But though they rejoiced in the nest they kept,
One had to be versed in country things
Not to believe the phoebes wept.

Robert Frost

"The Need of Being Versed in Country Things"

The house had been infected by the suburbs.
I heard the barn beside it heave a sigh
anticipating usufruct; or else decline,
decay, a sagging and senility;
or, worse, more merciless, a careless match
to send it up in flames like Mary Brown.
Nobody knows how much to make of barns
that do not shelter anything we value.
The crops are spent that went to Haskell's Mill.
This land has turned too sour even for hay
and lies now unprotected by the walls
that run and stumble, madmen, through the woods
which no one cuts or culls. Why are our barns,
that do not shelter anything we value,
left standing as an emblem of a past
when we owned things we thought more worth the keeping?

Peter Davison
From "Barn Fever"

The barns of the Dutch farmers were broad and
capacious. The roof, like that on their houses, was very
heavy, and sloped to within eight or ten feet of the ground.
There were holes near the roof for the barn swallows that
flitted in and out....Through the chinks of broken shingles
the rays of the sun fell across the darkness as if to winnow
the dust through the long shafts of light, or, where the
crevice was on the shady side, the daylight glittered through
like stars, for there were no windows in these barns: there
was light sufficient when the great double doors, large
enough to admit a load of hay, were open.

Gertrude Lefferts Vanderbilt
*The Social History of Flatbush and Manners and Customs of the Dutch
Settlers in Kings County*

The barn stood for shelter
      on squared corners with a tight roof
until the wind sucked it up
and spit it out in a shambles
of splintered boards. I tried
to salvage the ruins. While I
pulled the nails and sorted out
split studding, citizens of the
barnyard clustered around—pigeons
fluttered where once the ridge pole
hung, sparrows frisked through
broken window frames—and let me sweat
over the collapse of order.
I lit my pipe and tossed the match
toward the tumbled hay and let
chance decide if it lived or went out.
The flame caught, winked among the
stems, then tongued the air until
the draft formed a chimney and the
fire went mad. I leaned against a
corner post, the roar of the fire like music,
the lunge of its appetite now
beyond control.

James Hearst
"Destruction"

. . . In the country especially, nothing can be more fun or more appropriate than a barn dance, or an impromptu play, or a calico masquerade, with properties and clothes made of any old thing and in a few hours—even in a few minutes.

Music need not be an orchestra but it must be *good*, and the floor must be adequate and smooth. The supper is of secondary importance. As for manners, even though they may be "unrestrained," they can be meticulously perfect for all that! There is no more excuse for rude or careless or selfish behavior at a picnic than at a ball.

Emily Post
Etiquette: The Blue Book of Social Usage

C attle were found
  frozen stiff in the barns
by farmers this morning.

New York Evening Post
January 28, 1904

L eft over straw
  Fresh meadow hay

Worn wooden stalls

Work horse harness

Split reins

Roping reins

Single broken reins

Bridles with geometric bits

Spider webs

Curry combs

Kid saddles

Old saddles

Trophy saddles

Halters and ropes

Horses stomping and munching

Grain

Meowing, leaning cats.

Dad, though gone, comes alive when I step into my barn.

Sandra Mann
"Barn Bridges"
In memory of her father, Parmer Helmer (1911–1969)

Fern Mullins and Cy had, the evening
before, driven alone to a barn-dance in
the country. (Carol brought out the
admission that Fern had tried to get a
chaperon.) At the dance Cy had kissed
Fern—she confessed that. Cy had obtained
a pint of whisky; he said that Fern had
given it to him; Fern herself insisted that he
had stolen it from a farmer's overcoat—
which, Mrs. Bogart raged, was obviously a
lie. He had become soggily drunk. Fern had
driven him home; deposited him, retching
and wabbling, on the Bogart porch.

Sinclair Lewis
Main Street: The Story of Carol Kennicot

Old Baltus Van Tassel was a perfect picture of a thriving, contented, liberal-hearted farmer. He seldom, it is true, sent either his eyes or his thoughts beyond the boundaries of his own farm; but within those every thing was snug, happy, and well-conditioned. He was satisfied with his wealth, but not proud of it; and piqued himself upon the hearty abundance, rather than the style in which he lived. His stronghold was situated on the banks of the Hudson, in one of those green, sheltered, fertile nooks, in which the Dutch farmers are so fond of nestling. A great elm-tree spread its broad branches over it; at the foot of which bubbled up a spring of the softest and sweetest water, in a little well, formed of a barrel; and then stole sparkling away through the grass, to a neighboring brook, that bubbled along among alders and dwarf willows. Hard by the farmhouse was a vast barn, that might have served for a church; every window and crevice of which seemed bursting forth with the treasures of the farm; the flail was busily resounding within it from morning to night; swallows and martins skimmed twittering about the eaves; and rows of pigeons, some with one eye turned up, as if watching the weather, some with their heads under their wings, or buried in their bosoms, and others swelling, and cooing, and bowing about their dames, were enjoying the sunshine on the roof.

Washington Irving
The Legend of Sleepy Hollow

They have been painting the barn red and white...chasing skunks from the stage, clearing bird nests from the spotlights, scraping mildew from costumes and very gingerly, in the manner of city slickers, shooing snakes out of the yard.

Maureen Dowd
"On managers of summer theaters"
New York Times, June 18, 1984

E very mile on our route
today has given some
new occasion to admire the
scale upon which farming is
conducted in Pennsylvania...
the barns into which their
harvests are gathered are so
spaciously and solidly built.
that they want only
architectural design to rival
in appearance the most
ambitious private mansions.

Charles Fenno Hoffman
A Winter in the West

The North wind doth blow and we shall have snow
And what will poor Robin do then, poor thing?
He'll sit in the barn to keep himself warm
And hide his head under his wing, poor thing.

Mother Goose
"The North Wind"

The warm spring weather, together with these disappointments, bred in me the desire to roam. I packed away my traps and started for Buffalo with my grip, walking along the lake. It set in with a drizzling rain, and I was soon wet to the skin. Where the Chautauqua summer school grounds are now I surprised a flock of wild ducks near the shore, and was lucky enough to wound one with my revolver. But the wind carried it out of my reach, and I trudged on supperless, through Mayville, where the lights were beginning to shine in the windows. Not one of them was for me. All my money had gone to pay back debts to my Dexterville landlady. The Danes had a good name in Jamestown, and we were all very jealous of it. We would have starved, every one of us, rather than leave unpaid debts behind. As Mrs. Ben Wah many years after put it to me, "it is no disgrace to be poor, but it is sometimes very inconvenient." I found it so when, worn out with walking, I crawled into an abandoned barn halfway to Westfield and dug down in the hay, wet through and hungry as a bear. It stormed and rained all night, and a rat or a squirrel fell from the roof on my face. It felt like a big sprawling hand, and woke me up in a great fright.

The sun was shining upon a peaceful Sabbath when I crawled out of my hole and saw to my dismay that I had been sleeping in a pile of old hay seed that had worked through and through my wet clothes until I was a sight. An hour's patient plucking and a bath in a near-by pond restored me to something like human shape, and I held my entry into Westfield.

Jacob August Riis
The Making of an American

The barn was pleasantly warm in winter when the animals spent most of their time indoors, and it was pleasantly cool in summer when the big doors stood wide open to the breeze. The barn had stalls on the main floor for the work horses, tie-ups on the main floor for the cows, a sheepfold down below for the sheep, a pigpen down below for Wilbur, and it was full of all sorts of things that you find in barns: ladders, grindstones, pitch forks, monkey wrenches, scythes, lawn mowers, snow shovels, axe handles, milk pails, water buckets, empty grain sacks, and rusty rat traps. It was the kind of barn that swallows like to build their nests in. It was the kind of barn that children like to play in. And the whole thing was owned by Fern's uncle, Mr Homer L. Zuckerman.

E. B. White
Charlotte's Web

"Mr Creede has said that you can tell us where our taxes have gone. We shall be glad to be set right if we are laboring under a mistake and doing your county government any injustice. We shall be glad to have you tell us in a general way, where our taxes HAVE gone. What have you to show for these very heavy levies upon our properties? Our mission here is to find that out."

Mr Upright, having finished his dinner, shoved back his chair, wiped his beard and rose.

"Perfectly natural question," said he, with another sly and unobserved wink at Mr Creede. "Deserves a frank answer. I can't say what the other boys have to show for 'em; but as f'r me, I've got a good house, an' a damn good barn. Good day. See you ag'in, I hope!"

Herbert Quick
The Hawkeye

From the loft of the barn, or from the little platform on top of the windmill, I could look north into the Great Plains and do some serious daydreaming.

Larry McMurtry
Walter Benjamin at the Dairy Queen

For sixty years the pine lumber barn
had held cows, horses, hay, harness, tools, junk
amid the prairie winds...
and the corn crops came and went, plows and wagon
and hands milked, hands husked and harnessed
and held the leather reins of horse teams
in dust and dog days, in late fall sleet 'til the work
was done that fall.
And the barn was a witness, stood and saw it all.

Carl Sandburg
From "The People, Yes"

I took a walk with my wife, around the trout pool and over against the hill. The air was chill and the wind blowing from the north had winter in it. We listened for frogs, but they had shacked up for the winter. But we heard a coyote howl upwind and we heard a cow bawling for her late weaned bairn. The pointers came to the wire mesh of the kennel, wriggling like happy snakes and sneezing with enthusiasm, and even the sickly one came out of his house and fleered at us. Then we stood in the high entrance of the great barn and smelled at the sweetness of alfalfa and the bready odor of rolled barley. At the corral the stock horses snorted at us and rubbed their heads against the bars, and Specklebottom took a kick at a gelded friend just to keep in practice. Owls were flying this night, shrieking to start their prey, and a nighthawk made soft rhythmic whoops in the distance.

John Steinbeck
Travels With Charley

Arn-monat. Anglo-Saxon.
œrnmonath, barn month.
The Anglo-Saxon name for August,
because it was the month for
garnering the corn.

E. Cobham Brewer
Dictionary of Phrase and Fable

Blazing in Gold and quenching in Purple
Leaping like Leopards to the Sky.
Then at the feet of the old Horizon
Laying her spotted Face to die;

Stooping as low as the Otter's window,
Touching the Roof and tinting the Barn,
Kissing her Bonnet to the Meadow,—
And the Juggler of Day is gone!

Emily Dickinson
"Blazing in Gold and quenching in Purple"

Bok next decided to see what he could do toward eliminating the hideous bill-board advertisements which defaced the landscape along the lines of the principal roads....Bok now called upon his readers in general to help by offering a series of prizes totaling several thousands of dollars for two photographs, one showing a fence, barn, or outbuilding painted with an advertisement or having a bill-board attached to it, or a field with a bill-board in it, and a second photograph of the same spot showing the advertisement removed, with an accompanying affidavit of the owner of the property, legally attested, asserting that the advertisement had been permanently removed. Hundreds of photographs poured in, scores of prizes were awarded, the results were published, and requests came in for a second series of prizes, which were duly awarded.

Edward William Bok
The Americanization of Edward Bok: The Autobiography of a Dutch Boy Fifty Years After

A stable-lamp is lighted
   Whose glow shall wake the sky;
The stars shall bend their voices,
And every stone shall cry.
And every stone shall cry,
And straw like gold shall shine;
A barn shall harbor heaven,
A stall become a shrine.

Richard Wilbur
From "A Christmas Hymn"

Archie and Nick continue inseparable. I wish you could have seen them the other day, after one of the picnics, walking solemnly up, jointly carrying a basket, and each with a captured turtle in his disengaged hand. Archie is a most warm-hearted, loving, cunning little goose. Quentin, a merry soul, has now become entirely one of the children, and joins heartily in all their plays, including the romps in the old barn. When Ethel had her birthday, the one entertainment for which she stipulated was that I should take part in and supervise a romp in the old barn, to which all the Roosevelt children, Ensign Hamner of the *Sylph*, Bob Ferguson and Aleck Russell were to come. Of course I had not the heart to refuse; but really it seems, to put it mildly, rather odd for a stout, elderly President to be bouncing over hay-ricks in a wild effort to get to goal before an active midget of a competitor, aged nine years. However, it was really great fun.

Theodore Roosevelt
"A President at Play; Letter to Miss Emily T. Carow, Oyster Bay, August 16, 1903."
Theodore Roosevelt's Letters to His Children

He had driven half the night
From far down San Joaquin
Through Mariposa, up the
Dangerous mountain roads,
And pulled in at eight a.m.
With his big truckload of hay behind the barn.
With winch and ropes and hooks
We stacked the bales up clean
To splintery redwood rafters
High in the dark, flecks of alfalfa
Whirling through shingle-cracks of light,
Itch of haydust in the sweaty shirt and shoes.
At lunchtime under Black oak
Out in the hot corral,
—The old mare nosing lunchpails,
Grasshoppers crackling in the weeds—
"I'm sixty-eight" he said,
"I first bucked hay when I was seventeen.
I thought, that day I started,
I sure would hate to do this all my life.
And dammit, that's just what
I've gone and done."

Gary Snyder
"Hay for the Horses"

Other examples of the application of old words to new purposes are afforded by *freshet*, *barn* and *team*. A *freshet*, in eighteenth century English, meant any stream of fresh water; the colonists made it signify an inundation. A *barn* was a house or shed for storing crops; in the colonies the word came to mean a place for keeping cattle also. A *team*, in English, was a pair of draft horses; in the colonies it came to mean both horses and vehicle.

H. L. Mencken
The American Language

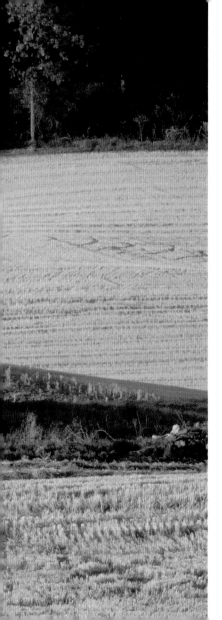

But a barn is also a cathedral where visiting town-boys come to worship farm life. It has the well-rubbed wood of a reverenced church rail, the grain raised by the protuberant hides of quietly agnostic cows. In the hayloft you learn the meaning of motes and beams. You walk across its plank floor, head tilted back. Day outside finds cracks in the roof and walls of the hayloft, and light streaks through the darkness on missions of grace and accusation. The barn is wired to God's wrath by a lightning rod.

Verlyn Klinkenborg
Making Hay

13 And one of the company said unto him, Master, speak to my brother, that he divide the inheritance with me.

14 And he said unto him, Man, who made me a judge or a divider over you?

15 And he said unto them, Take heed, and beware of covetousness: for a man's life consisteth not in the abundance of the things which he possesseth.

16 And he spake a parable unto them, saying, The ground of a certain rich man brought forth plentifully:

17 And he thought within himself, saying, What shall I do, because I have no room where to bestow my fruits?

18 And he said, This will I do: I will pull down my barns, and build greater; and there will I bestow all my fruits and my goods.

19 And I will say to my soul, Soul, thou hast much goods laid up for many years; take thine ease, eat, drink, *and* be merry.

20 But God said unto him, *Thou* fool, this night thy soul shall be required of thee: then whose shall those things be, which thou hast provided?

21 So *is* he that layeth up treasure for himself, and is not rich toward God.

The Holy Bible, King James Version
"The Parable of the Rich Fool,"
The Gospel according to St. Luke 12, 13-21

barn ₁ *n.* **1** a large farm building for storing grain etc. **2** *derog.* a large plain or unattractive building. **3** *US.* a large shed for storing road or railway vehicles. **barn dance 1** an informal social gathering for country dancing, originally in a barn. **2** a dance for a number of couples forming a line or circle, with couples moving along it in turn. **barn-owl** a kind of owl, *Tyto alba*, frequenting barns. [Old English *bern*, *beren* from *bere* barley + *ern*, *ærn* house]

barn ₂ *n.* *Physics* a unit of area, 10^{-28} square metres, used esp. in particle physics. ¶ Symb.: **b**. [perhaps from phrase "as big as a barn"]

The Oxford Encyclopedic English Dictionary

Borden, Lizzie Andrew
1860–1927, American woman accused of killing her father and her step-mother. b. Fall River, Mass. The elder Bordens were hacked to death with an ax on Aug. 4, 1892. Although Lizzie Borden claimed that she was out in the barn at the time, she was accused of the murders and tried. The trial, which aroused great public interest, ended with a verdict of not guilty. The case was never solved.

Columbia Encyclopedia

Regarding an 1864 incident in Hell Gate. George Shears…was hanged in a barn near the store. The rope was thrown over a beam, and he was asked to walk up a ladder to save the trouble of preparing a drop for him. "Gentlemen." he said. "I am not used to this business. Shall I jump off or slide off?" He was told to jump.

Harold G. Merriam
Montana: A State Guide Book
(The WPA Guide to Montana)

Through the ample open door
   of the peaceful country barn,
A sun-lit pasture field, with cattle and
   horses feeding;
And haze, and vista, and the far horizon
   fading away....

Walt Whitman
From "A Farm Picture"

Index of Authors

Acknowledgments

Note: Every effort has been made to contact current copyright holders. Any omission is unintentional, and the publisher would be pleased to hear from any copyright holders not acknowledged below.

p.11 From "A Barn is More Than a Building. It's a Shrine to our Agrarian Past," by Jim Doherty (*Smithsonian Magazine*, August 1989). Copyright © 1989 by Jim Doherty. Used by permission of the Author. **p.12** "Nebraska, Early March" by William Kloefkorn. Reprinted from *Prairie Schooner*, vol. 60, no. 2 (summer 1986). Used by permission of the University of Nebraska Press. Copyright © 1986 University of Nebraska Press. **p.14/72** From *Charlotte's Web* by E. B. White. Copyright © 1952 by J. White. Reproduced by permission of Penguin Books Ltd. **p.19** Quoted material from Randy Leffingwell's *The American Barn* used with permission of MBI Publishing Company: www.motorbooks.com **p.20** From *The Grapes of Wrath* by John Steinbeck (Penguin Books, 2001). Copyright © 1939 by John Steinbeck. Reprinted by permission of Penguin Books Ltd. **p.33** "Portrait of a Figure Near Water." Copyright © 1996 by the Estate of Jane Kenyon. Reprinted from *Otherwise: New & Selected Poems* with the permission of Graywolf Press, Saint Paul, Minnesota. **p.39** "Cleaning the Barn" by James Hearst from *Snake in the Strawberries* (Iowa State University Press, 1979). Copyright © 1979 Iowa State University Press. Reprinted with permission from the University of Northern Iowa Foundation. **p.47** "The Need of Being Versed in Country Things" from *The Poetry of Robert Frost* edited by Edward Connery Lathem. Copyright © 1923, 1969 by Henry Holt and Company, copyrighted © 1951 by Robert Frost. Reprinted by permission of Henry Holt and Company, LLC. **p.49** "Barn Fever" from *Barn Fever* by Peter Davison, published by Secker & Warburg. Used by permission of The Random House Group Limited. **p.52** "Destruction" by James Hearst from *Snake in the Strawberries* (Iowa State University Press, 1979). Copyright © 1979 Iowa State University Press. Reprinted with permission from the University of Northern Iowa Foundation. **p.55** From *Etiquette: The Blue Book of Social Usage* (Funk and Wagnalls Company, 1928). By permission of the Emily Post Institute, Inc. **p.58** "Barn Bridges" by Sandra Mann. By permission of the Author. **p.60** From *Main Street: The Story of Carol Kennicot* by Sinclair Lewis, copyright © 1920 by Harcourt, Inc. and renewed 1948 by Sinclair Lewis. Reprinted by permission of the publisher. **p.64** From "On Managers of Summer Theaters" by Maureen Dowd, *The New York Times*, June 18, 1984. Copyright © 1984 by The New York Times Co. Reprinted by permission. **p.74** From *The Hawkeye* by Herbert Quick. Copyright © 1923 by The Curtis Publishing Company and Herbert Quick, renewed © 1951 by Ella Corey Quick. Reprinted with the permission of Scribner, an imprint of Simon & Schuster Adult Publishing Group. **p.78** From "The People, Yes" by Carl Sandburg. Copyright © 1936 by Harcourt, Inc. and renewed 1964 by Carl Sandburg. Reprinted by permission of the publisher. **p.80** From *Travels With Charley* by John Steinbeck (Penguin Books, 1992). Copyright © 1962 by John

Steinbeck. Reprinted by permission of Penguin Books Ltd. **p.89** From "A Christmas Hymn" in *Advice to a Prophet and Other Poems*. Copyright © 1961 and renewed 1989 by Richard Wilbur. Reprinted by permission of Harcourt, Inc. **p.93** "Hay for the Horses" from *Riprap and Cold Mountain Poems* by Gary Snyder. Copyright © 1990 by Gary Snyder. Reprinted by permission of North Point Press, a division of Farrar, Straus and Giroux, LLC. **p.94** From *The American Language* by H. L. Mencken (Knopf, 1999). By permission of Random House Inc. **p.97** From *Making Hay* by Verlyn Klinkenborg (The Lyons Press, 1986.) By permission of the Author. **p.98** From the *Authorized Version of the Bible* (The King James Bible), the rights in which are vested in the Crown, are reproduced by permission of the Crown's Patentee, Cambridge University Press. **p.100** From The Oxford Encyclopedic English Dictionary edited by Joyce M. Hawkins and Robert Allen (1991). Reprinted by permission of Oxford University Press.

Photo Credits

First edition for North America published in 2003
by Barron's Educational Series, Inc.

MQ Publications Ltd
12 The Ivories
6-8 Northampton Street
London N1 2HY
United Kingdom

Anthologist: Wynn Wheldon
Design: Philippa Jarvis
Editor: Leanne Bryan

All inquiries should be addressed to:
Barron's Educational Series, Inc.
250 Wireless Boulevard
Hauppauge, NY 11788
http://www.barronseduc.com

Library of Congress Catalog Card No.: 2002111569

International Standard Book No.: 0-7641-5581-4

Printed in China
9 8 7 6 5 4 3 2 1